Metamorphosis
Nature's Magical Transformations

Alvin Silverstein
and
Virginia Silverstein

Dover Publications, Inc.
Mineola, New York

For Jean Karl

Bibliographical Note

This Dover edition, first published in 2002, is a slightly emended republica-
tion of *Metamorphosis: The Magic Change*, originally published by Atheneum,
New York, 1971.

Library of Congress Cataloging-in-Publication Data

Silverstein, Alvin.
    Metamorphosis : nature's magical transformations / Alvin Silverstein and
Virginia Silverstein.
        p. cm.
    Originally published: New York : Atheneum, 1971.
    Summary: Describes the process of metamorphosis, the change from larva
to adult, in such animals as frogs, butterflies, and honeybees.
    ISBN 0-486-42396-4 (pbk.)
    1. Metamorphosis—Juvenile literature. [1. Metamorphosis.] I. Silverstein,
Virginia B. II. Title.

QL981 .S55 2002
571.8'76—dc21

2002074161

Manufactured in the United States of America
Dover Publications, Inc., 31 East 2nd Street, Mineola, N.Y. 11501

Contents

Metamorphosis:
The Magic Change

Our world is ever changing. It is cold in the winter and warm in the summer. It rains one day, and the sun is out the next. Sometimes changes are very slow—so slow we do not notice them. It takes many millions of years for a mountain to wear away. Sometimes changes are very fast. Have you ever noticed how quickly the little puddles on a wet street dry up when the sun comes out after a shower?

Living things change too. Children grow bigger and bigger each day, until one day they are as big as their parents. But as they grow, they change mostly in size, not in shape. They already look much like their mothers and fathers. They have two eyes, two ears, a nose, a mouth, two arms, and two legs, just as their parents do.

"Of course this is true," you may say. "Don't all children look like their parents?" Many do. A kitten looks like a little cat. A puppy looks like a little dog. A baby bird, with its beak and wings, looks very much like its parents. Even a baby grasshopper is much like its mother and father.

But some babies do not look at all like their parents. If you saw a wormlike caterpillar, unless you knew, you would never think that it would grow up to be a beautiful butterfly, with large, brightly colored wings. A tadpole, just a big head and a long, swishing tail, does not look at all like its tail-less, hopping parent frogs.

For a tadpole to turn into a frog, or a caterpillar to turn into a butterfly, a wondrous series of changes must take place. The baby must become almost a new animal before it can be like its parents. This change is called metamorphosis.

Metamorphosis is found in many different kinds of animals. Some of these are rather close relatives, and so it is to be expected that they would grow and develop in much the same way. Most insects, for example, go through two very different stages of life after they hatch from the egg. But some of the animals that go through a metamorphosis come from very different groups, groups that are not closely related at all. The eggs of a variety of water animals hatch into small swimming creatures that have to go through enormous changes, both inside and out, before they are like their parents; and the adult forms, such as sea squirts, star-fish, and eels, have almost nothing in common with each other, except that they are all animals.

Why do some kinds of animals go through such tremendous changes during their lives, while others, like humans, merely grow in size from infants to adults? Scientists believe that the plants and animals that now live on our earth are the result of a long process of development, stretching back for millions and even billions of years. Long ago, when the earth was young, some simple forms of life appeared and multiplied. Some of their children were slightly different from the parents, much as you are probably a little different from your parents, even though you resemble them in many ways. Once in a while, one of these differences gave a particular creature a small advantage over the other creatures of the world—perhaps it could find more food or have more young or live in places that other creatures could not. This creature would probably live longer and have more descendants than its brothers and sisters. Among its descendants there would again be some that were slightly different, and the best adapted ones of these would thrive and multiply. Gradually a great variety of life forms appeared and spread through the waters and lands of the earth.

During this long evolution, creatures changed not only in shape, but also in ways of life. The ones that survived and multiplied were those that could best meet the needs of the environment in which they lived. A water animal had to have some means of swimming; or, if it stayed in one place, some way of attracting food to it. It had to have some way to separate out the tiny amounts of oxygen dissolved in the water; its means of breathing had to be very different from the lungs of an animal that breathes air. An animal living in a cold climate had to have some way of keeping warm, or some other way to get through the winter without dying of the cold. An animal living in the desert had to have ways of saving its precious small supply of water. The many different kinds of animals that have survived to our time have found many different answers to the problems of their lives. Most birds and bats and insects have wings that permit them to fly through the air. Flying helps them find homes and food, and sometimes to escape from winter's cold. But if you look closely at birds and bats and insects, you will find that their wings are built quite differently. Each form of life represents one set of answers to a particular group of problems. They may not be the only answers. They may not even be the best possible answers. But they work, well enough to permit the creatures to survive.

And so it is with metamorphosis. The animals whose lives include these enormous changes in shape and ways of living have found a set of answers that gives them some special advantages in the struggle for life. Metamorphosis is not the only answer—other kinds of animals facing the same types of problems merely grow in size as we do. But for bees and frogs and starfish, and an enormous number of other animals, metamorphosis is a way of life that works.

Butterflies and Moths:

Nature's Sleeping Beauties

On a warm summer day in the country, sweet smells fill the air. Dotted over the green fields are bright-colored flowers of many kinds and many shapes. Here and there a bee buzzes about, stopping now and then to sip some nectar or gather a bag full of pollen. And bright-winged butterflies flit from flower to flower. Later, as the sun sets and twilight deepens into the darkness of night, it is the turn of the moths to flutter about.

As a butterfly or moth alights on flower after flower, it sips sweet nectar through a long sucking tube, which is really a sort of tongue. The insect usually carries this sucking tube curled up under its face, but the tube can uncurl to reach all the way to the bottom of the petal vase. As the butterfly or moth perches on a bloom, tiny bits of dustlike pollen cling to its body. Then the insect alights on other blooms of the same kind. It recognizes them by their color and smell. Pollen brushes off from its body onto the new blooms. In this way the plant becomes pollinated and can make seeds, so that new plants can grow up the next year.

There are more than 120,000 different kinds of moths and butterflies, each with its own special colors and shape. They belong to more than 70 different families.

Moths and butterflies are very much alike in many ways. They all have bodies divided into three parts, and they have six legs and four wings. Their large

Attacus caesar, *one of the world's largest moths, measures 10½ inches from wing tip to wing tip. U.S.D.A. Photograph.*

wings are covered by rows of tiny colored scales, which overlap like the shingles of a roof. Although the night-flying moths are usually paler in colors than the day-flying butterflies, some moths are brightly colored too. One way to tell moths and butterflies apart is by their antennae—the two long "feelers" that grow out from the tops of their heads. Butterflies' antennae are usually long and slim, with knobs or clubs at the ends. Moths' antennae look like a pair of feathers or fern leaves. Butterflies and moths usually hold their wings differently when they rest, too. Generally a butterfly will fold its wings up, and a moth will hold them out flat.

But butterflies and moths both go through a series of almost magical changes during their lives. For the young are so different from the adults that it is hard to believe they are the same kind of insect.

In the spring or early summer the adults of these insects mate. Male and female butterflies and moths find each other in much the same way that they find just the right flowers to suck nectar from—by color and especially odor. These insects smell with their antennae, and their sense of smell is wonderfully sharp. When a female is ready to mate, she sends out special odors, which are carried through the air by the breezes, and a male will follow her scent, sometimes for miles,

Butterfly egg mass. U.S.D.A. Photograph.

until he reaches her. A swarm of males may be attracted to one female, and then they may fight to mate with her.

The male and female fly together, and the male places his seed—millions of tiny sperm cells—inside the female's body. There the sperms join with her small egg cells, fertilizing them and starting the lives of new butterflies or moths.

Now the mother is ready to lay her eggs. With her keen sense of smell, she picks out a plant and places them there. The plant that she chooses is just the right kind of plant for her babies to eat when they hatch. Each kind of butterfly and moth has special plants on which it and its young prefer to feed. Depending on what kind of butterfly or moth the female is, she may lay only one egg at a time or may lay bunches of eggs together. One kind of butterfly or moth may attach her eggs to a leaf; another may string a necklace of eggs around a twig.

But wherever the eggs may be, each one will soon hatch out into a small, wriggly, wormlike creature, a caterpillar. Scientists call it a larva. It does not look like a butterfly or moth at all. It has no wings. Most caterpillars have eight pairs of legs, spread out along their wormlike bodies. Many caterpillars are greenish and match the leaves and stems they crawl upon. But some are quite brightly colored, with gaudy spots or stripes. Some, like the caterpillar of the spicebush swal-

Monarch Butterfly larva.
Alvin E. Staffan from the National Audubon Society.

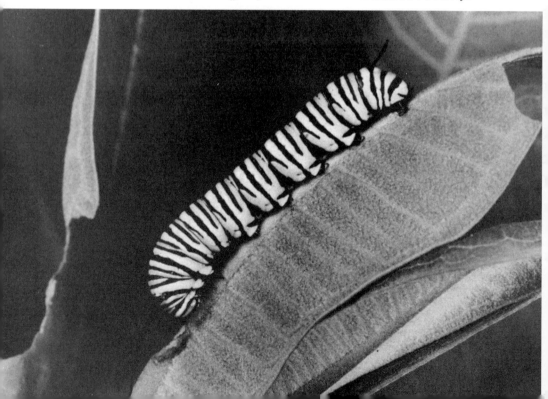

owtail butterfly, even have a pair of big false eyes, which may frighten their enemies.

The caterpillar, or larva, has an enormous appetite. It may eat up the leaf on which it was born. Then it will crawl along the stem or branch, looking for more leaves to eat. It does little but eat all day. Soon the caterpillar is so fat that its skin is almost bursting. For a caterpillar's skin is not like ours. It is made of a tough substance called chitin, which is as rigid as a suit of armor. The insect would not be able to move at all if its chitin skin did not have a great many joints. And chitin skin cannot grow. Once it hardens, it will stay the same shape and size.

Yet a caterpillar does grow. It eats until it has no more room inside its suit of armor. Then its skin splits open, very much like a sleeping bag unzipping. The caterpillar wriggles out, and leaves its old skin behind. This is called molting.

Under its old skin, the caterpillar has grown a whole new skin. But when the creature has just molted, the new chitin is still soft. It takes a few minutes to harden. Quickly the caterpillar breathes in as much air as it can hold and puffs its body up. This makes a larger frame for the new skin to harden over, and leaves some room for the larva to grow inside.

After it has molted, the caterpillar begins to eat again. It grows and sheds its skin several more times.

But each time, the creature that wriggles out of the out grown skin is still a caterpillar. It does not yet look a all like a butterfly or moth.

Suddenly the caterpillar stops eating. It is not ill instead, special chemicals inside its body are at last pre paring it for the changes of metamorphosis.

The caterpillar now spins out some silk from a silk making gland in its body. It first makes a small ball o silk, with which it attaches the hind end of its body to a leaf or stem. The caterpillar of a butterfly may also spin a line of silk that it loops around the middle of it body and anchors to the twig. It is something like the safety belt around the waist of a telephone lineman climbing up a telephone pole.

Caterpillars of moths usually spin out still more silk and wrap strands of it around and around their bodies until they are completely covered. This silken cover ing is called a cocoon. Though the silk is light, it i very strong. It will keep the insect snug and protected through the long, cold winter while metamorphosis i taking place.

Though caterpillars of most butterflies do not spin cocoons, they do have a protection too. As the cater pillar is settling down on the twig it has chosen, it molt for a last time. Its new skin is a hard tough case, called a chrysalis case. This case may be clear enough to see the body of the insect inside, or it may be green o rown, blending with the plants or soil. Or it may be narked with gold or silver, which sparkles in the sun. The word *chrysalis* comes from a Greek word meaning *golden*.

Inside a cocoon or a chrysalis, the caterpillar is not a caterpillar any more. In this new stage of life it is called a pupa. The pupa does not move. Nothing seems to be happening. But marvelous changes are taking place.

The body of the pupa seems to melt, until it is almost liquid inside. Then it begins to take new shapes. Large new eyes replace the small eyes of the caterpillar. Six long, thin insect legs take the place of the short, stubby caterpillar legs. Long, delicate feelers grow out from the pupa's head. And on its back buds sprout, which gradually grow out into two pairs of wings, closely wrapped and folded about the insect's sleeping body.

The pupa stays wrapped in its cocoon or chrysalis case until the weather turns warm again, or until it is time for it to come out. Then the sleeper stirs, makes a little hole in its cocoon or case, and wriggles out.

The pupa stage is finished. The insect has become an adult. But the creature that emerges from the cocoon or case still does not look like a moth or butterfly. It is damp and pale, with crumpled tissue-paper wings. The warm sun and the breeze little by little complete the

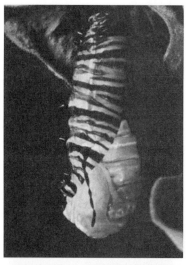

The skin of the Monarch Butterfly larva folds rapidly upward, showing one third of the chrysalis case Louis Quitt from the National Audubon Society.

Monarch Butterfly chrysalis case. John H. Gerard from the National Audubon Society.

Monarch Butterfly pupa two hours before hatching. Harry Brevoort from the National Audubon Society.

Monarch Butterfly just emerged from its chrysalis case.
Alvin E. Staffan from the National Audubon Society.

changes of metamorphosis. The insect darkens and dries, and its crumpled wings begin to spread out like bright-painted fans.

At last, a butterfly or moth perches for a moment on the empty shell it has just left, stretching and shaking out the wrinkles in its wings, and then flutters off. It may live for only a few weeks, or it may live for nearly a year. But before it dies it may find a mate and start off a new generation, which will go through the same cycle—from egg to caterpillar, to pupa, and at last adult—all over again.

The life of a butterfly or moth is almost like two lives. The chubby caterpillar crawls along the ground and up the stems of plants to reach its supply of food. It cannot move very fast or far, but it does not need to. For the caterpillar is a sort of eating machine: Most of its life is made up of eating and growing and storing up energy. Then, as the pupa rests within its cocoon or chrysalis case, the stored energy is used to build a whole new animal—the adult moth or butterfly.

How different the life of the butterfly is from the life of its earthbound larva. The adult can fly through the air for miles, sampling the breezes for faint scents that tell it where to find food and a mate. A caterpillar might bumble about on the ground for days without ever meeting another of its kind. But a butterfly or moth can range far over the countryside, guided by its keen sight and smell. After mating, the female can fly off to seek a field or forest where there will be a plentiful supply of food for her children, and there she will lay her eggs.

The Honeybee:

A Pampered Baby

One of the best cared for babies in the living world is
the honeybee larva. From the very moment that the
pearly little egg is laid by the queen mother of the hive,
there are workers bustling about to see to its every
need.

For the honeybee baby does not grow up alone, as
butterfly larvae do. It is born into a busy hive, filled
with thousands of bees, each with its own special job
to do. There are worker bees who go out into the fields
to gather sweet nectar and pollen from the flowers to
make into food. Other worker bees stay in the hive
and do many tasks. Some keep the hive clean and neat;
others build the comb—rows and rows of tiny six-sided
chambers or cells molded from wax that the bees make
themselves. Some worker bees turn nectar into thick,

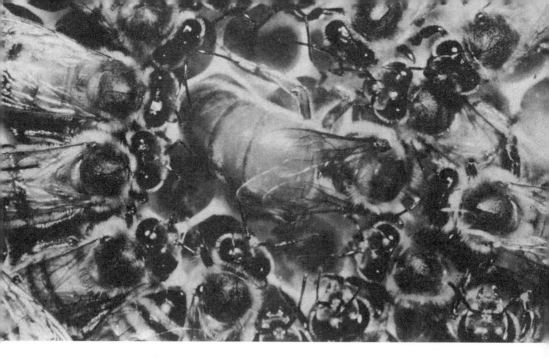

The honeybee queen. Courtesy of the Carolina Biological Supply Co⌐

sweet honey, and others mix nectar and pollen to form
a nourishing food called beebread. And a special group
of workers are nurse bees, who care for the young of
the hive and feed them a special "bees' milk" called
royal jelly.

All the eggs are laid by a single large bee, the queen.
She is the mother of the whole bustling family of the
hive. She and all the worker bees are females. The only
males in the hive are a few hundred drones. These lazy
fellows just wander around the hive all day. They can
not even feed themselves. But one of them may one day
mate with a new queen and help to start off a new gen
eration of bees.

Mating generally takes place in the fall. As the hive grows crowded at the end of the summer, an unusual excitement stirs. The queen and a group of workers fly out of the hive to seek a new home. After the old queen has left, the nurse bees choose a new queen from among the growing princesses in the hive. Soon she flies out on her marriage flight, with a swarm of drones winging after her. The fastest, strongest drone meets the new queen high in the air and mates with her. Sperm cells from the male are placed inside a special sac within the queen's body, and there she will keep them for several years, as long as she reigns as queen in the hive. The drone, his one task completed, crumbles to the ground, dead. Meanwhile the young queen flies back to the hive, to take up her duties there.

The queen bee is fed and cleaned and protected by a little band of workers. For the queen has only one job to do—lay eggs for the hive. She places each egg she lays in one of the small wax cells of the comb. The eggs that will grow into worker bees are fertilized with sperm that the queen received from the drone on her marriage flight. These worker eggs are placed in small cells. The eggs that will be drones are laid in slightly larger cells. When the queen lays one of these drone eggs, she keeps the sperm pouch within her body tightly closed, so that these eggs are not fertilized at all. In some mysterious way, at just the right time of year,

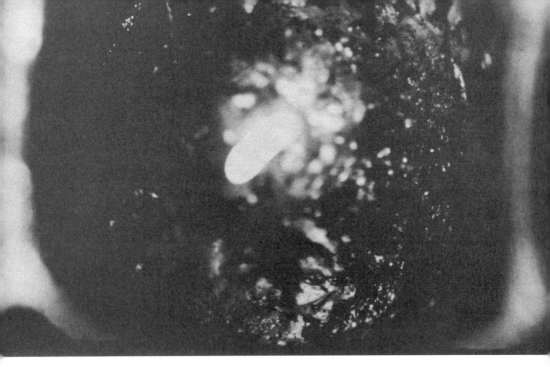

The honeybee egg. Courtesy of the Carolina Biological Supply Company.

Honeybee brood cells.
Courtesy of the Carolina Biological Supply Company.

Honeybee larva.
Courtesy of the Carolina Biological Supply Company.

The worker bees choose a few of the fertilized eggs to raise as queens. These eggs are placed in special, very large cells.

When the wiggly little larvae first hatch out in their wax cells, each has a tasty meal of royal jelly waiting for it. Greedily it gobbles down its food. Before it has a chance to get hungry again, a nurse bee bustles up with still more food. She will feed it and clean it and fuss over it, just as your mother did for you when you were a baby.

After a few days, the little larva is fed solid food instead—the cakes of nectar and pollen called beebread. (But the larvae chosen to be queens are still fed royal jelly every day for a whole week.) The wriggling little

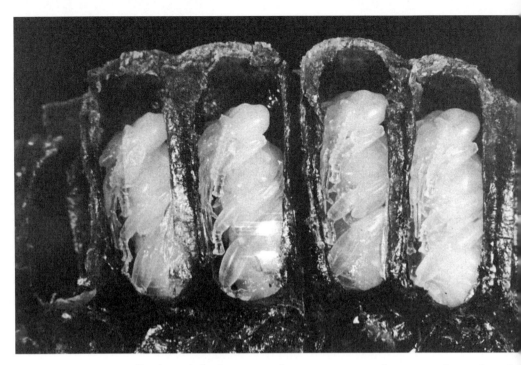

Section of the honeycomb cut away, exposing young honeybees in their cells. Lynwood Chace from the National Audubon Society.

larva grows larger and larger and has to shed her skin a number of times as she gobbles the food that her busy nurses bring her. But she still does not look at all like a bee. She looks like a fat little white worm.

For about five and a half days the honeybee larva eats and grows. Then, when she has grown so large that she almost fills her nursery cell, a curious thing happens. She spins herself a silken cocoon and curls up to sleep. Now the busy nursemaids put a tight wax cover over her cell and seal her up. For almost two weeks the honeybee larva will stay locked inside her little cell. She will not eat at all. But strange and wonderful changes are taking place. The bee larva has now become a pupa and soon will be a bee.

Eyes are growing where there were none. Legs and wings appear—all neatly folded to fit inside the cocoon.

For a while the almost-bee is pearly white. She looks like a little statue of a bee, molded in wax. But soon her eyes begin to darken. Then her body turns a lovely blend of gold and black.

Finally the full-grown honeybee is ready to waken. Out of her cell she comes, ready to join her sisters in the busy hive. There, unless it is autumn, she will live and work for about six weeks before she dies. If it is autumn, she will live through the winter with the queen. All the drones die after the mating flights in the fall. But the queen and enough workers live on from year to year to keep the hive going and to start new hives. And so the cycle of larva, pupa, and adult bee goes on.

Honeybee pollination.
Courtesy of the Carolina Biological Supply Company.

The Dragonfly:

Life in Two Worlds

For butterflies, bees, and many other insects, metamorphosis means a change from a slow-moving larva that does little but eat and store energy to a winged creature that can fly through the air to find a mate and a new home. But for the dragonfly, metamorphosis brings an even more amazing change. In the course of its life, this insect lives in two completely different worlds.

The dragonfly's life begins in the watery world of the pond. There, in the stalk of a cattail or other water plant, just below the surface, a mother dragonfly has made a double row of tiny holes. In each hole she has placed a tiny egg. For three weeks the eggs have been growing and changing. And then at last the baby dragonflies are ready to come out into the pond.

The little dragonfly that emerges from one of the

toles is not much bigger than the head of a pin. He does not look like a dragonfly: his body is short and stubby, and he is colored pale green and brown, just like the plant to which he is clinging. But he has a much more complicated shape than a bee larva or a moth caterpillar. He has a definite head, with eyes and a mouth and a very large lower lip folded across the lower part of his face like a bandit's mask. And he is quite clearly an insect, for he has six long legs. In fact, the baby dragonfly looks so much like a full-grown insect that it would not seem right to call him a larva. Yet he does not look at all like his parents, and never would if all he did were to grow in size. The sweeping changes of metamorphosis will be needed before he will become a true adult dragonfly. So scientists use a different name for the young of dragonflies and other insects that develop in the same way: They call them nymphs.

The dragonfly nymph does not pause long to look about at the watery world of the pond. Soon he is crawling along the plant stem looking for food. For like the bee and butterfly larvae, the young dragonfly nymph will eat and eat, stuffing himself until his chitin skin is so tight that he must shed it in order to grow.

At first the dragonfly nymph will feed on the many microscopic creatures that live in the pond. When he grows larger, he will be able to catch larger prey—worms and smaller nymphs of other insects. He catches his food in a most unusual way. Stalking his prey as a lion does in the jungle, the dragonfly nymph creeps quietly along the stem or leaf of a water plant until he is within striking distance. Then suddenly, his neatly folded lower lip opens up and shoots out like a trap. Two pointed hooks at the end of the lip snap together like pincers and snare an unwary pond creature. Then the lip folds up again and pulls the prey into the dragonfly nymph's mouth.

But life in a pond is a dangerous one, even for an animal armed with such an effective weapon. Larger nymphs are prowling about, looking for food. Giant water bugs and diving beetles have enormous appetites too. All of them can make a meal of a dragonfly nymph. But the dragonfly nymph has a trick that sometimes helps him to escape his enemies. Some of the water that he swallows is held in a large chamber in his abdomen. If the dragonfly nymph squeezes hard with the muscles of his abdomen, the water goes spurting out through an opening in the rear of his body. The water comes out so forcefully that it pushes his body forward. And so the dragonfly nymph can go shooting through the water in just the same way that a jet plane flies through the air. If he moves faster than his pursuer, he escapes.

The dragonfly nymph is entirely a water creature. The water chamber inside his abdomen is lined with rows of gills, very much like the gills of a fish. Using

Dragonfly nymph. Lynwood Chace from the National Audubon Society.

Dragonfly nymph catching fish. Robert Hermes from the National Audubon Society.

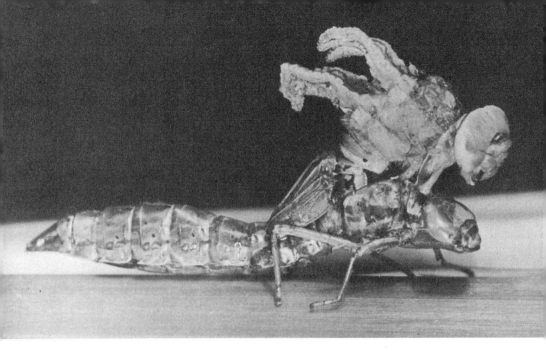

Dragonfly breaking out of its nymph stage.
Lynwood Chace from the National Audubon Society.

The dragonfly completes his final molting.
Robert Hermes from the National Audubon Society.

these gills, he can take in oxygen from the water. And so, just like a fish, the dragonfly nymph never has to go up to the surface to breathe.

As the days go by, the dragonfly nymph prowls about the pond, searching for food. He eats and grows, taking in more than his own weight of food each day. Soon he is large enough to attract the attention of fish and frogs. But if he succeeds in escaping from them, he will grow large enough so that he, in turn, will be able to feed on small fish and tadpoles. As the nymph grows, he must molt again and again. In the first few molts, he just grows larger. But after the fourth molt a little bump appears on his back. With each molt that follows, the bump grows larger. The dragonfly is changing. But this clumsy, humpbacked creature still does not look like a dragonfly.

At last, almost a year after his egg was laid, the dragonfly nymph is ready to complete his metamorphosis. He stops eating and remains for a few days clinging tightly to the stem of a water plant. Inside his body, the final changes are taking place. When all is ready he climbs up the stalk of the plant, out of the water for the first time in his life. Now the last molt begins. A rip appears on the back of the humpbacked nymph, and as he wriggles and stretches, the tear spreads until it is large enough for him to struggle out. There he perches on his old skin, a slender dragonfly

31

at last. But he is pale and soft, and his wings are crumpled.

Gradually the warm sun and gentle breeze dry the skin of the young dragonfly. His body darkens, and his wings turn to glistening gauze. This time of drying is a time of danger, when the darting tongue of a frog or the swooping bill of a bird might snap up the helpless insect. But at last the drying is completed. The dragonfly spreads his wings and swoops up into the sky.

Now the dragonfly is a creature of the land and the air, and in this new world he finds a new way of life. In one way it is very much like the old one—he is constantly hungry and must hunt for food. As he swoops through the air, he peers about him with large gleaming eyes. Each of them is made of a thousand tiny lenses, which see even the smallest bit of possible food. Back and forth and up and down the dragonfly turns his eyes; he can even see behind him. As he flies, he keeps his six legs cupped together to form a sort of basket. In this basket, like a sort of fishing net, he catches mosquitoes, moths, and other insect prey.

Then one summer day, while flying near a pond, the dragonfly spies another of his kind. It is a female. They meet in midair and, still in swift flight, they cling together and mate, then part. Soon the female will alight on one of the water plants growing up from the pond. Down the stalk she will crawl—the only time she will

The adult dragonfly.
Jeanne White from the National Audubon Society.

ever return to the water in which she spent the first year of her life. There, underwater, she will drill neat holes in the plant stalk and lay a single egg in each. Then she will fly away, never to see the young nymphs that will emerge from the holes and begin the cycle again.

Frogs and Their Cousins

Each spring, when the last snows have melted away and the weather is growing warm, life of many kinds awakens after the long quiet of winter. Everywhere tiny shoots push up through the ground, and the fields and meadows turn green. The quiet ponds are suddenly bustling with life. Birds sweep low over the water to take their morning bath or catch their breakfast from the swarms of insects that have hatched from winter eggs. Schools of fish weave here and there. And deep in the mud at the bottom of the pond, frogs awaken from their winter's sleep and come up to swim and hop about.

As the weather grows warmer, the frogs begin to look for mates. Early in April, spotted leopard frogs begin to call to each other around the pond. Later in

The mating clasp of the male and female frogs.
Courtesy of the Carolina Biological Supply Company.

the season, perhaps in June or July, depending on how far north it is, it will be the turn of the large bullfrogs to begin croaking their mating call.

During the mating season, especially at night, the air is filled with a chorus of croaks, as male frogs call to the females. Soon females begin to answer and join the males. Then it is time to mate.

A pair of frogs swims about in the pond together. The male swims just behind the female, clinging tightly to her sides, and holding on with special rough patches on his fingers. As he clasps her, the female lays her eggs, thousands of them, which spread out like a cloud in the water. Then the male spreads his own sperm cells over the eggs, and there in the water the eggs are fertilized. Many of the tiny swimming sperms meet eggs; and as a sperm and an egg join, the life of a new frog is started off.

Each of the eggs laid by the female has a coat of a jellylike substance around it. As the eggs float in the water, the jelly swells, and the eggs stick together, forming a floating mass that looks rather like tapioca. The egg mass floats along in the water until it bumps into waterweeds or clumps of reeds growing near the edge of the pond. There it clings, as changes begin to take place within the eggs.

At first, perhaps an hour after the eggs are laid and

Close-up of frog eggs showing tiny tadpoles inside.
C.G. Maxwell from the National Audubon Society.

fertilized, each egg looks like a tiny ball, dark on top and white underneath. It is surrounded by the ball of jelly, clear enough to see right through.

As the days go by, small fishlike animals take shape inside the balls of jelly. In five or six days they are ready to hatch. Out they come, wriggling little creatures, with big rounded heads and a long, flattened tails. They do not look at all like their parents. Instead, they look like small greenish fish. They are now tadpoles or polliwogs. Some day they will be frogs. But many changes must take place first.

For a long while the little tadpoles do not seem to be changing very much at all. They swim about in the pond, feeding on small bits of green plant life and growing larger and larger. They are very much like fish in many ways. They do not have any legs. And they must stay in the water all the time, for they do not have lungs for breathing air. Instead, they breathe through gills on the sides of their heads, just as fish do. Water that the tadpole takes in through its mouth passes out through its gills, where the oxygen in the water passes into its bloodstream.

While the tadpoles are small, there are many dangers for them in the pond. They have no teeth or other weapons with which to defend themselves; all they can do if an enemy is near is to try to swim away. Many tadpoles are eaten by fish, such as pike and trout. Even large water insects may kill tadpoles. Dragonfly nymphs have specially hinged jaws that they can shoot out like a trap to catch their prey. The giant water bugs have needle-like snouts, with which they suck the body fluids from smaller animals such as tadpoles. So many tadpoles are killed, that of the thousands of eggs laid, perhaps only a few hundred grow large enough to begin to change into frogs.

Just how long a tadpole grows before it begins to show signs of the strange changes of metamorphosis varies depending on the kind of frog. The tadpoles of small frogs, like the leopard frog, begin to change in about two and a half months. Bullfrogs take much longer; it is two full years before an egg becomes a bullfrog. The time needed for the change also depends on the weather—the warmer it is, the more quickly the tadpoles grow and change.

The change itself is a very fascinating thing to watch. Two little knobs or buds appear near the back of the tadpole's head, one on each side, close to where the head joins the tail. With each passing day the buds grow larger. Soon they begin to look like legs, at first short and stubby, then longer with webbed toes. These are hind legs, and the tadpole is quite funny looking at this stage. It has a big head and a tail and a pair of long hind legs, but no forelegs at all can be seen. Then, in a week or two, two more buds appear, farther for-

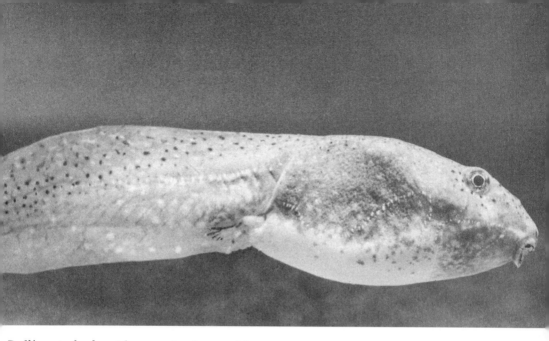

Bullfrog tadpole with sprouting legs and feet.
George Porter from the National Audubon Society.

ward. Within days they grow into perfectly formed
forelegs.

The little tadpole is looking more and more like a
frog. And amazing changes are going on inside its
body, too. It is growing a pair of lungs, very much
like the lungs that humans have, and its gills are begin-
ning to disappear. Within its mouth, teeth are growing. And its stomach and intestines are changing. A
tadpole has very long intestines, which work to digest
the green plant life on which it feeds. But a frog does
not eat plants at all. It feeds on insects and other animals, which are easier to digest. Now the tadpole's intestines begin to grow shorter.

Tadpole in last stage before becoming a frog.
Stephen Dalton from the National Audubon Society.

These are upsetting changes for the tadpole. Inside and outside, it is being transformed from a fishlike, swimming creature, which feeds on green plants and breathes with gills underwater, to a frog, which will breathe air into its lungs, hop about on land, and catch insects and other animal prey. For a while it is neither one nor the other—no longer really a tadpole, but not yet quite a frog. It can no longer digest the plant life it once ate, but it is not yet able to catch animal prey. And so the tadpole stops eating. But it does not starve. It has a source of food stored away in its body—in its tail. The almost-frog begins to digest its own tail and

Bullfrog.
H. Charles Laun from the National Audubon Society.

use it for energy. Each day the tail grows shorter, until at last it disappears.

Finally the change is complete. For leopard frogs, it has been more than three months since the eggs were laid. Of the thousands of eggs that floated in the pond, perhaps less than a hundred are left; many tadpoles have been eaten by hungry fish, water bugs, and snakes. One by one, the little frogs that remain crawl out of the water. They breathe in air for the first time with their new lungs (their gills have entirely disappeared). They hop about and explore their new world. They catch insects with flicks of their lightning-fast tongues.

All the rest of the summer and into the fall, the young frogs stay near the pond or stream where they were born. They spend the warm days eating and sunning themselves and diving into the water at the first sight or sound of danger approaching. There are still many dangers in the life of a frog; and many are eaten by birds or snakes or animals like raccoons that often hunt for food by the water.

The young frogs that survive eat and grow. When cold weather comes, they bury themselves deep in the mud at the bottom of the pond. All their body processes slow down; they do not need to eat, and the little breathing that they do, is done through their wet skin and brings them all the oxygen that they need. The frogs are hibernating. They sleep the winter away, safe far below the sheet of ice that covers the pond. In the spring they awake and take up their life by the side of the pond once more. Again they eat and grow larger, for they are not yet adults. But though they change in size, never again will the frogs go through a series of changes as great as those of their metamorphosis.

At last, in the spring when they are two or three years old, or even older in the case of bullfrogs, the grown frogs mate and lay eggs of their own.

The frogs' cousins, toads and most salamanders, also start their life as tadpoles. They too must go through a series of changes very similar to those of the frog be-

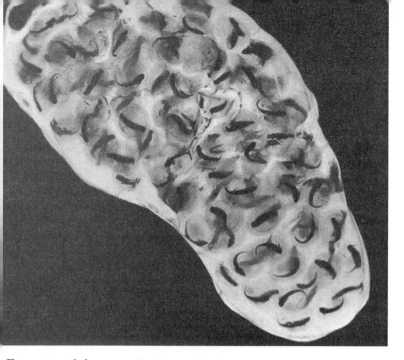

Egg mass of the spotted salamander.
George Porter from the National Audubon Society.

fore they are fully grown.

But not all young salamanders grow up in the same way that a frog does. Some finish all their changes while they are still in the egg. When they hatch, they look like small copies of their parents.

Other salamanders never really grow up at all. These are the axolotls that live in Mexico. Though they have legs and a tail like an adult salamander, they never grow a pair of lungs. Instead they always keep their feathery gills and stay in the water all their lives.

Scientists believe that salamanders like the axolotls once went through a metamorphosis just as their relatives do. In fact, scientists can make axolotls grow up.

43

Axolotl salamander.
A.W. Ambler from the National Audubon Society.

Dusky salamander guards its eggs under a rock.
Hal H. Harrison from the National Audubon Society.

If a chemical called thyroxin is added to the water in which the axolotls live, in a short time they will lose their feathery gills and grow lungs. Then these salamanders can breathe air and live on land.

In the metamorphosis of frogs and their relatives we may see today how long, long ago, creatures that had once spent all their lives in the sea gradually came to move out onto the land. Some animals became totally adapted to life on the land, but others, like the frog, did not, and still need water to survive during at least parts of their lives.

The Sea Squirt:

The Tadpole That Isn't

Let's take a trip to the seashore on a warm summer day. We walk along the wet sand, and the waves come in every now and then and ripple over our feet. Here and there we pick up a pretty shell, or dig after a little clam- or crablike creature that scrambles back into the sand as the water retreats.

Wading out a bit farther, we find other living things. If we stand very quietly and do not move, shining minnows dart between our legs. We may also find some small creatures that look just like tiny tadpoles swimming about. We have to look very closely to spot them, for they are very small indeed, and their bodies are almost transparent.

At certain seasons of the year, swarms of tiny "tadpoles" can be found swimming about in nearly all the

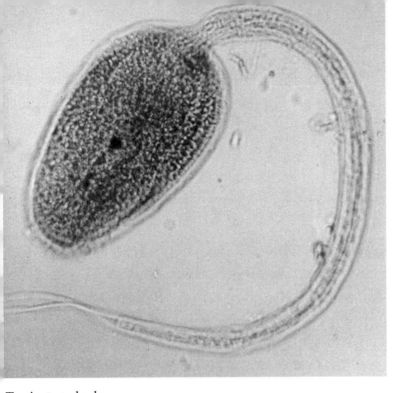

Tunicate tadpole.
Photograph by Lorus and Margery Milne.

oceans of the world, from the clear bright waters of the tropics to the icy waters near the poles. But they are not *real* tadpoles and will not turn into frogs one day, for tadpoles are not found in the sea. They live only in fresh water—in ponds and lakes and streams.

The little "tadpoles" of the ocean swim about with great ease, for their long tails send them gliding through the water. They rush and play about near the surface of the water. Then a strange thing happens. Their tails begin to wag less and less, and soon they stop moving altogether. Slowly the little creatures sink to the ocean bottom. They have had less than a day to play.

47

What has happened to the little "tadpoles"? Are they going to die? No, they are simply about to begin their metamorphosis. Soon each "tadpole" attaches itself to a rock on the ocean bottom with three special suckers on the front of its head. There it stays, upside down, firmly fastened to the bottom. And then it starts to change.

The little animal's tail begins to disappear. It becomes shorter and shorter as the creature's body grows plumper and plumper and twists about into a letter U, with what were its two ends pointing upward. Even queerer changes are taking place inside the body. The little eyes, which helped the "tadpole" to swim toward the light near the surface of the water, are disappearing. So are its tiny ears, which helped it to keep its

Sea squirt.
Robert Hermes from the National Audubon Society.

balance when it was swimming. The long cord of nerves, which passed down its back very much like our spinal cord, disappears too, leaving only a tiny brain. But its throat, which is covered with thousands of tiny openings, like a strainer, grows bigger and bigger until it almost fills the animal's body. And on the outside of its body, the animal forms a thick, tough covering called a tunic.

When these changes have all taken place, the little animal does not look at all like a tadpole any more. It looks like a little round barrel, with two funnel-shaped "mouths," out of which it may poke two long, hollow tubes. It sucks water in through one tube and squirts it out the other. The ocean "tadpole" has not turned into a frog; it has become a sea squirt.

Tunicate, or sea squirt, with an attached tubeworm seen at the top. William M. Stephens / EKOS.

What a dull life the adult sea squirts live. Their day of swimming freely through the ocean is over forever. Once they have attached themselves to rocks or seaweed at the bottom of the sea, they never move again. They grow larger and come to look like brightly colored rubbery bags. They hardly seem like animals at all. They have no eyes or ears or tails. They never grow arms or legs or fins. Even their tough, baglike coverings are made of something very much like cellulose, the stiff substance that keeps plant leaves and stems and roots plump and firm. All these strange animals ever do is suck in water, strain out tiny bits of food through the strainers inside their bodies, and squirt the water out again. And one day they mate and give rise to baby sea squirts, tiny "tadpoles" of the ocean that begin the amazing changes of metamorphosis all over again.

Another name for sea squirts is tunicates, because of the tough coverings, or tunics, that they form around their bodies. Tunicates come in many different sizes, shapes, and colors. There are blue sea squirts and green ones and purple ones, yellow ones and orange ones. Some sea squirts are called sea peaches, because they are just about the size, shape, and color of a ripe peach. Other sea squirts, which live together in clusters on rocks or old pilings along the Atlantic Coast of the United States, are called sea grapes. Like grapes, these

50

Ciona intestinalis or tube sea squirts.
Photograph by Lorus and Margery Milne.

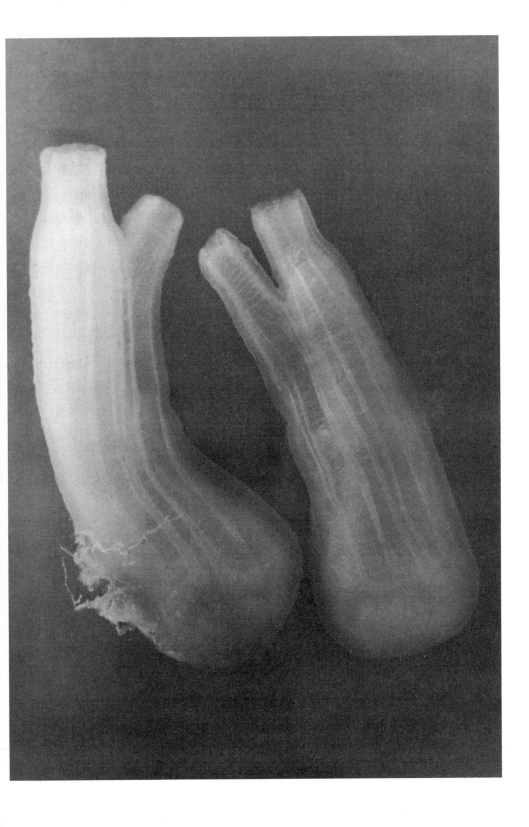

sea squirts are small and round, and greenish-yellow colored.

One of the strangest types of sea squirts is called *Pyrosoma*, which means "fire body." The bodies of these sea squirts make a living light; they glow like fire in the water. Hundreds or even thousands of these animals grow together in a very odd way. Instead of attaching themselves to the bottom of the ocean, they fasten their bodies together to form a long, hollow tube, closed at one end. Each of the creatures has one "mouth" facing out into the sea and another pointing into the hollow part of the tube. As the sea squirts of the group suck water in through their outside "mouths" and squirt it out through their inside "mouths," a stream of water flows out through the open end of the tube. This sends the colony slowly swimming along, by a very gentle sort of "jet propulsion."

Like the axolotls, which are salamander tadpoles that never grow up, there are also a few kinds of tunicates that never change from their tadpole-like swimming form. One of these has a very curious way of life. It makes a slimy stuff, which it forms into a little "house" shaped like a lemon. It uses this small house as a place to hide and as a trap for bits of food. But in a few hours, the slimy trap becomes clogged with bits of sand and dirt and other things that are not good to eat. So then the tunicate must leave its house and make itself a new one.

The Starfish:

Star of the Sea

It is hard to believe that the beautiful five-armed starfish is a vicious killer, hated by many fishermen. In many parts of the world, fishermen raise oysters and clams to harvest for tasty shellfish dinners. But starfish, too, love to eat oysters and clams. They crawl about on the ocean bottom catching these shellfish. The starfish grasps the shells of its victim and pulls and pulls. The clam or oyster tries to keep its shells shut tight. Indeed, it can keep itself so firmly closed that a man cannot open it without a knife.

But the starfish is a patient animal. It wraps its five arms around the shells of the clam. Two arms pull on one side with many small suckerlike feet, and the other three arms pull on the other side. The starfish pulls slowly but steadily, hour after hour. At first nothing

53

Giant tropical starfish.
Photograph by William M. Stephens/EKOS.

seems to happen—the clam seems determined to stay shut. But then the clam begins to tire, and at last it opens up, perhaps just a tiny crack. But that is enough.

For then a strange thing happens. The starfish can turn its stomach inside out. Out flows the starfish's stomach, right out of its mouth and through the narrow opening in the clam's shells. The starfish digests its meal inside the clamshell, as juices from its stomach turn the clam's body into a soupy liquid. Then the starfish brings its stomach back into its body and sucks up its already-digested meal.

Starfish are very greedy. They may eat a half dozen or more clams or oysters in a day. No wonder the fishermen do not like them and kill them whenever they can.

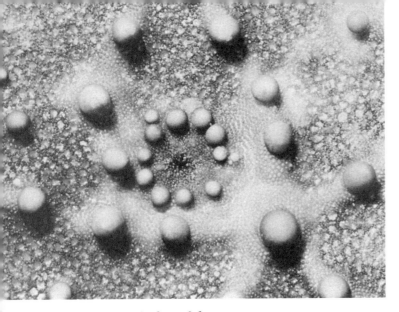

Mouth of the giant tropical starfish.
William M. Stephens/EKOS.

For many years, whenever an oysterman caught a starfish, he chopped it up into pieces and threw them back into the sea, thinking that it was a good way to get rid of the pest. But the poor fisherman did not know what he was doing. For the starfish has wonderful powers of healing. If an arm is cut off, it can grow a new arm. In fact, an arm that is cut off can sometimes grow into a whole new starfish. So when an oysterman cut one of these five-armed pests into pieces and threw them into the water, many of the pieces grew into new starfish. The oysterman was not killing the hated pests at all; he was actually making more of them.

But starfish have a better way of making more of themselves. Eggs from the female starfish and sperm from the males mix in the water, and from the fertilized

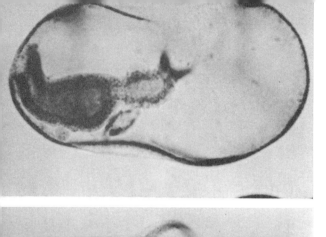

Early starfish larva. Courtesy of the Carolina Biological Supply Company.

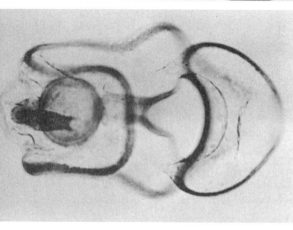

Starfish larva view from underneath. Courtesy of the Carolina Biological Supply Company.

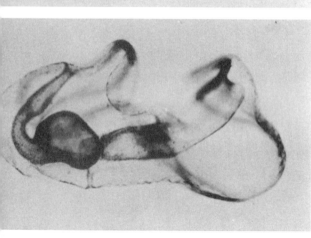

Starfish larva side view. Courtesy of the Carolina Biological Supply Company.

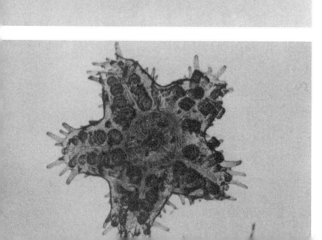

Young starfish. Courtesy of the Carolina Biological Supply Company.

eggs baby starfish come to be and start to grow. These baby starfish look nothing like their parents. They do not have five arms like the points of a star—they do not have any arms at all.

The baby starfish look rather like knobby little kidney beans, with a small mouth and rows of tiny hairs called cilia that wave back and forth and help them to swim through the water. For a while they swim about and feed on little bits of green plant life.

After a few weeks each little larva settles to the bottom and attaches itself to a rock with a special sucker that grows near its mouth. There it stays for awhile without moving. But marvelous changes are taking place inside. Its mouth closes forever, and a new one opens up in a different place. Five little arms appear where there were none, and the part of its body where its mouth once was seems to melt away.

Soon there is a five-pointed star, so small that it could sit on the tip of your thumb. But how hungry it is! It crawls away from its rock in search of tiny clams to eat. It will eat and grow with each passing day. Soon it will be a full-sized orange or brown or purple or green starfish, crawling about on the bottom of the sea.

The starfish has many relatives that also live on ocean bottoms around the world. The brittle stars look like other starfish except that they have long, slender arms, which can bend and coil about as smoothly and easily as the long body of a snake. They are called brittle stars because when one is picked up or disturbed by an enemy, it literally seems to fall apart. One or even all of its arms break off, and then break into pieces distracting the enemy. What is left is just the middle part of the brittle star. It crawls off, and in time the missing arms grow back.

Other relatives of the starfish, the sea lilies and feather stars, look like lovely sea flowers. They have long, feathery arms. The sea lily spends its adult life attached by a long, slender stalk, like the stem of a flower, to a rock or piling on the ocean bottom. Feather stars also have stalks at first, but soon break away and then swim about by flapping their long arms.

The sea urchin and the sand dollar, also relatives of the starfish, are quite different. Their round bodies are enclosed in a hard shell of lime and covered with spines, which they can move back and forth. Sea urchins look like round pincushions. Sand dollars are quite flat, like the coins they are named after.

Even more different are the sea cucumbers, whose long, leather bodies look like cucumbers or sausages lying on the ocean bottom. Like the brittle star, the sea cucumber has an unusual way of distracting its enemies. If it is disturbed, it shoots out many long, sticky tubes that tangle about the fish or crab or other sea creature that disturbed it. If a sea cucumber is disturbed even more, it may go farther—it may actually turn itself partly inside out and shoot out most of the inside of its body. Then it breaks away and crawls off, leaving its own body organs wriggling about before the enemy. Within a month or two, the sea cucumber will have grown new organs.

These relatives of the starfish seem quite different from one another. But they all go through the same amazing kind of metamorphosis as their starfish cousin.

Sea cucumber in the foreground, two sea urchins and a sea star to the left, feather duster worm, center, and a feather star, right. Photograph by Lorus and Margery Milne.

Eels:

Fish Like Snakes

The ocean is vast and deep. Men in mighty ships have often lost their way while traveling far from land. Yet many sea creatures seem able to navigate without difficulty in the ocean waters with no maps or compasses to guide them. They can travel thousands of miles and find their way to just the right places, even if they have never been there before.

Among the water creatures that can steer so well through the oceans are the eels. They spend much of their lives in freshwater streams and ponds in Europe or America, eating and growing. For many years fishermen wondered why all the eels they caught were large ones; there never seemed to be any eggs or young eels about. It was not until the end of the last century that scientists began to piece the story together. And even now much mystery remains.

When the female eels are about five feet long and the males are about two feet long, they are ready to begin the long and dangerous journey that will take them from their freshwater homes to their mating grounds. They have lived in their river homes for years, as slender yellowish or brown fish, so long and thin that they look almost like snakes. They have been

A neon goby picks parasites from the head of a large green moray eel. William M. Stephens/EKOS.

The Atlantic moray eel swims with a serpentine motion.
William Stephens / EKOS.

sleek and fat, but suddenly, they stop eating. Their bodies turn a silver gray, and their eyes grow larger. Down the streams and rivers they start, swimming toward the sea. At last they reach the edge of the deep and salty Atlantic Ocean. But they do not stop there. Into the ocean they swim, and on and on, for hundreds and even thousands of miles. Most fish would die if they went from fresh water into salt water. But not the eels. On they swim, until at last they reach the warm, still waters of the Sargasso Sea. This is where

62

they will mate and then die. And this is where swarms of eggs that have been laid deep in the water will hatch out into baby eels.

Though some of the eels have come from America, and others have come all the way from Europe, each will mate only with its own kind. Soon after the eggs are laid, the Sargasso Sea is swarming with baby eels. But they do not look like eels at all.

The larvae that hatch from the masses of eggs that the mother eels lay in the water look like tiny flat fish. Each baby eel is as clear as glass—so clear that the inner parts of its body can be seen right through its skin. These eel larvae are so different from their parents

Eel larva, Leptocephalus, *captured in a deep plankton net in the Sargasso Sea, the area of the Atlantic Ocean where the eels spawn. William M. Stephens/EKOS.*

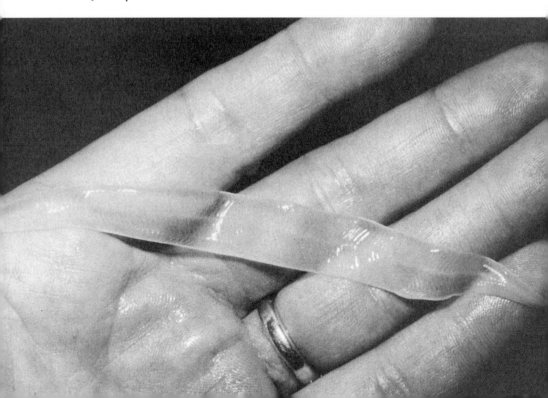

that the first scientists who caught some did not even realize that they were young eels. They thought that the small creatures were a kind of ocean fish and gave them a name all their own: *Leptocephalus brevirostris,* which means "leaf-headed short nose." Eventually it was discovered that these little fish were really young eels, and gradually more was learned about their life story.

The tiny larvae eat and grow as they swim about in the ocean. And soon they begin a journey of their own. The ocean currents carry them off toward the mainland. For some reason, one that scientists still do not entirely understand, the larvae that hatched from eggs laid by American eels are carried toward the coast of the United States, while the young of the European eels drift off toward Europe. The larvae of the American eels travel west from the Sargasso Sea for more than a year, until they reach the homeland of their parents. Their European cousins must take an even longer journey to reach their home. For about three years they drift eastward in the Gulf Stream, eating and growing. The lucky ones avoid being eaten by larger fish.

All these little larvae are saltwater fish. They could not live in the fresh water of the streams from which their parents came. But when they reach the coast of Europe or America, a change takes place. The little larvae, which have by now grown to be several inches

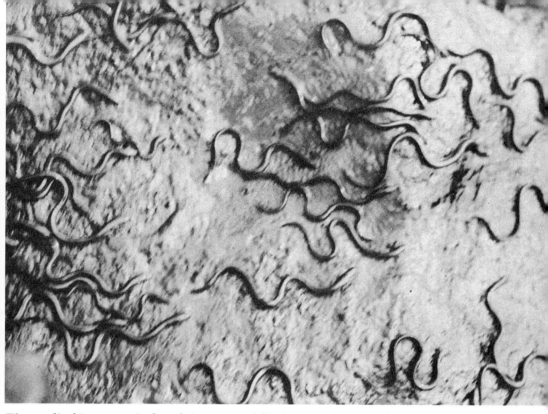

Elvers climbing a vertical rock in a waterfall after coming out of the ocean. Fred Lewis from the National Audubon Society.

long, stop eating. Soon they begin to look like eels. Their bodies become rounded and slender, but they are still transparent. At this stage they are called glass eels. Their metamorphosis is almost completed.

It is late autumn when the eel larvae reach the coast. By the following spring, they are ready to start up-river. Their glassy-clear skins turn dark, and they look just like little eels. They are not really larvae any more; instead they are elvers. And there have been changes inside their bodies too, which have made them able to live in fresh water. The males stay close to the river

Two eels in an aquarium tank.
Science News.

mouths, but the females swim far upriver, to make their homes in streams and ponds. There they will feed and grow, until at last they too feel the mysterious call that will send them on their long journey back to the ocean where they were born.

Metamorphosis:
Ways of Survival

We have followed the lives of seven different kinds of animals. The animals themselves are quite unlike one another, and their ways of life are very varied too. They are linked by only one thing: During the lifetime of each, the animal lives in two or more distinct forms, each of which is so different from the others that it is hard to believe that they are forms of the same creature. The first of these forms is transformed into the next by a series of enormous changes that together are called metamorphosis.

In each case metamorphosis answers certain needs in the animal's life. This process has quite different meanings in the lives of different species. The animal may be helped to use different parts of its environment to good advantage or to overcome disadvantages that may arise in a particular way of life.

The dragonfly spends the first part of its life in the water and the second part free to roam through the air. Each of these environments offers its own opportunities for finding food and shelter, has its own needs for life, and holds its own dangers that must be escaped. The changes of metamorphosis make it possible for the dragonfly to live successfully in both worlds and perhaps to endure and reproduce itself more succesfully than if it lived in one place alone.

For butterflies and moths, a life cycle including metamorphosis permits the animal to grow and reproduce effectively. The caterpillar eats and grows; the adult can fly about and find a mate more easily than the land bound larva. It can also fly off to settle in new areas. This can be a very important advantage if the insect's original home is becoming crowded, or if food is becoming scarce there. Even the pupa stage provides some advantages; safe within the tough case of the cocoon or chrysalis, the insect can survive under conditions that would kill either the larva or the adult: hot, dry summer months or the freezing cold winter.

The two-part life cycle of the honeybees fits perfectly into the bees' social way of life. The fat larva is little more than an energy-storing package. It has no responsibilities in the hive; it just lies in its wax cell and gobbles down the food that the nurse bees feed to it. But it remains a part of the hive, and after its metamorphosis, it becomes a strong-winged adult bee, able to take part in the duties of the group.

Scientists believe that the frogs' ancestors were water-dwelling, fishlike animals. The first frogs and their relatives gained the ability to come out on land and enjoy the opportunities for food and shelter there. But they still kept many ties to the water. A frog's lungs do not work very well, and it gets part of its oxygen by breathing through its skin. But for this kind of "breathing" to work properly, the frog's skin must stay moist. And so the frog must remain near the water where it can take a dip every now and then to keep from drying out. Frogs must also spawn or lay their eggs in water, as their fishlike ancestors did. And eggs laid in the water must develop into water creatures, if they are to survive. For frogs, metamorphosis thus provides the bridge between the water-dwelling young forms and the land-dwelling adults.

The metamorphosis of the eels also enables them to live in two very different environments during different parts of their lives. The leaf-shaped larvae, which are well adapted to live in salt water, change into freshwater elvers as their long migration brings them to the coast. Then, after years of living in fresh water, the eels change again to saltwater fish as they migrate back to the sea to spawn. What advantages there may be in a life lived in both salt and fresh water is hard to say. Perhaps the eels' strange life cycle is a reflection of past history, and metamorphosis provides a bridge between the sea, where life began, and the fresh waters of the land, to which it spread.

For sea squirts, a two-part life cycle provides a quite obvious advantage. Adult sea squirts live very nicely, attached to the sea bottom. All the food they need comes drifting to them in the ocean currents, and they never have to move. They have even solved the problem of getting together to mate by shooting their sperms and eggs out into the water. But then, if the young sea squirts immediately settled down to the bottom, the sea squirt colony would soon be so crowded that they would have to grow on top of each other. There would not be enough food to feed the huge crowds of sea squirts, all jammed into a small area. So instead, the tadpole-like swimming larvae of the sea squirts do not settle down immediately. They swim and drift with the ocean currents. By the time they are ready to change to adults and take up a place on the ocean bottom, they have been scattered over a wide area. In that way there is space and food for all.

The opportunity to spread over wider areas is an advantage that metamorphosis gives to a great variety of ocean animals, both slow-moving forms like the starfish and sea urchins, and animals whose adult forms never move, such as sea squirts, oysters, and barnacles.

Thus for a great variety of animals, and in many different ways, metamorphosis helps animals in the struggle for survival. A two-part life cycle is not the only way to solve the problems of existence; it is not the way that *our* ancestors used. But it has proved to be a very sucessful way of life for a large portion of the animal kingdom.

Glossary

antennae (an-TEN-nee)—an insect's "feelers"; long, thin structures on its head with which it feels and smells

axolotl (ax-o-LOT-ul)—a salamander-like animal that lives in
   Mexico and can reproduce without going through metamorphosis

caterpillar (CAT-er-pill-er)—the larva (immature form) of a
   moth or butterfly

cellulose (SELL-you-lohs)—a material found in the walls of
   plant cells, which helps to stiffen them

chitin (KITE-in)—a tough material that forms the outer shells
   or "skeletons" of insects

chrysalis (CRISS-a-liss)—the pupa stage of butterflies

cilia (SILL-ee-uh)—tiny hairlike structures that wave back and
   forth; used as organs of movement by some microscopic
   organisms

cocoon (co-COON)—a protective case formed by some insect
   larvae before entering the pupa stage; made from strands
   of a silky material, wrapped about the insect's body

drone—a male bee; he does no work in the hive

egg cell—a special cell produced by a female, which combines
   with a sperm cell produced by a male to form a new organism

elvers (EL-vers)—young eels after the glass eel stage; able to
   live in fresh water

evolution (ev-oh-LUE-shun)—the development of forms of life
   from earlier forms, with survival of forms best adapted to
   their environment

fertilization (fer-til-li-ZAY-shun)—the joining of sperm and egg
   to start the life of a new organism

gills—platelike or feathery breathing organs of water animals

glass eels—young eels just before the change to freshwater forms

73

hibernation (hye-ber-NAY-shun)—a sleeplike resting state in which some animals spend the cold winter months

larva (LAHR-vuh)—an immature form of an insect or other animal that must go through a metamorphosis before it will resemble its parents

leptocephalus larva (lep-toe-SEF-uh-lus LARH-vuh)—young eel just after hatching from egg; resembles a transparent, leaf-shaped fish

metamorphosis (met-uh-MORE-foe-sis)—a great change in form and structure as an animal goes from immature to adult stage

molting (MOLT-ing)—shedding of skin, feathers, or other outer covering

nymph (NIMF)—an immature stage in the development of some insects

pupa (PUE-puh)—the stage in insect development during which the larva or nymph, enclosed in a protective case, changes into the adult form

sperm cell—a special cell produced by a male, which joins with an egg cell produced by a female to form a new organism

tadpole—the larva of a frog or other amphibian

thyroxin (thye-ROX-in)—a chemical produced in the thyroid gland

tunic (TUE-nik)—the tough covering that protects the body of tunicates such as the sea squirt

tunicates (TUE-ni-kaytz)—sea squirts and other baglike sea animals that have tadpole-like larval forms